CADMOS DOG TRAINING

Good times
with older dogs

CADMOS

DOG TRAINING

Read
Learn
Know

DOROTHEE DAHL

Good times
with older dogs

Care, fitness
and health

CADMOS

Copyright © 2009 by Cadmos Verlag GmbH, Schwarzenbek
Copyright of this edition © 2009 by Cadmos Books, Great Britain
Layout: Ravenstein+Partner, Verden
Typesetting: Grafikdesign Weber, Bremen
Cover photo: Frank Fritschy
Printed by: Westermann Druck, Zwickau

British Library Cataloguing in Publication Data

A catalogue record of this book is available from the British Library.

Printed in Germany
ISBN 978-3-86127-972-3

Contents

Contents

Preface

At some point, anyone who is lucky enough to have a dog will face a very special time: their beloved four-legged friend's old age.

It is not always possible to say at what point ageing begins: there are differences between breeds, but there are also very different individuals. One dog may be able to run about right into old age and still love long walks with their owner; another of the same age may be content with their vantage point in the garden. Whatever the signs of old age in your dog, the friend who may have been your companion for many years deserves to be allowed to grow old with dignity.

Because many things change, dogs will have different needs that are specific to this phase of life. In this book you will learn how to ensure that your senior dog stays fit and healthy for as long as possible. You will receive valuable tips on feeding the elderly dog, dealing with behaviours that are typical of old age and communicating with canine seniors who can no longer see or hear so well.

This book aims to provide ideas on how to make your dog's later years particularly enjoyable and how to give them everything they need during this special phase of life.

A dog who can look back on many years deserves to receive especially loving care in the autumn and winter of their life. (Photo: Tierfotoagentur/ Fischer)

A special time: the dog's old age

Firm friends: these two have grown up and experienced many things together. (Photo: Tierfotoagentur/ Richter)

Just as it's fun to take a lively young dog into your home, living with an elderly dog is also something really special. In most cases, you will have enjoyed a long acquaintance, may have spent many years together, and may even be able to understand each other without words. If, however, you have decided to offer a senior dog a home, the new relationship can take on a special quality when the dog is already elderly. It is astonishing how laid-back and sensible old dogs can be, even if their life experiences so far have not been very pleasant. They are often content with very little, delighted to be in close contact with people and to have a cosy bed, and they no longer need to be taught the lessons that are necessary for a young dog.

In addition to other factors, breed and size influence a dog's life expectancy. The dachshund in this photo is still young and doesn't have a single grey hair. (Photo:Tierfotoagentur/ Richter)

Grey muzzles:
when dogs start to get old

As with humans, the process of getting older starts in different ways with individual dogs. Depending on the colour of the dog, a greying muzzle can occur at a relatively young age. A number of factors play a part in the ageing of dogs: average life expectancy for the breed, health, the conditions in which the dog is kept, and their individual physical and mental constitution. The care given to the dog likewise has a positive influence on life expectancy; particular attention should be paid to a balanced diet that allows the dog to stay slim, sufficient exercise, and dental care and regular check-ups by the vet.

A varying starting point:
breed and size

Dogs of different breeds reach a different age, on average. There are breeds that can get very old: for example, it's not unusual for a poodle, cocker spaniel or Chihuahua to reach the age of fifteen years or more. Other breeds, on the other hand, often die far too young by our estimation. It is often the case, for example, that an Irish wolfhound – the giant among sighthounds – or even a mastiff fails to reach an age of more than than five to eight years old. Generally,

Huskies are among the breeds that rarely show their age. In this team photo the leading dog at the front left (black-and-white Pinto) is already eleven and a half years old. This was his final sled-dog race before he went into well-earned retirement. His partner in the photo is precisely ten years younger. (Photo: Roppelt)

it can be said that bigger dogs will die younger than small ones. For example, dachshunds are among the breeds that can get very old; Jack Russell terriers also sometimes live to seventeen and older. Labrador retrievers, with an average life expectancy of approximately ten years, are in the middle range. There are exceptions: golden retrievers and Airedale terriers, which are among the larger dog breeds, occasionally reach the age of fifteen years. In the case of mongrels, a role is played by the breeds that make up the mix. Given, however, that an entirely new genetic make-up has occurred in each mongrel, it can be assumed that many factors with a negative influence – such as inbreeding – are no longer prevalent. Therefore, mongrels frequently reach a higher age than the breeds from which they originate.

In addition to breed and size, the stress and strain a dog is placed under also play a part in its life expectancy. A working border collie, whose breed actually has a relatively high life expectancy at thirteen to fifteen years, can be worn out as early as the age of eight to ten if placed under extreme strain. However, many factors need to be weighed up here, as an excessively fat dog who lazes about on the couch all its life will not, as could be predicted, reach an old age.

One small item of solace for the fact that a dog is unable to be a lifetime companion for us is that the life expectancy of our dogs has risen overall. This can be attributed both to improved medical care and treatment and to feeding that is tailored to the condition and age of the dog.

Is my dog old?

In order to establish whether your dog is already advanced in years, you should watch them closely every day. In addition to the grey hairs on the muzzle and at other points in the fur there are many signs that may hint that your dog is becoming a senior citizen. However, it is always important to clarify first that these signs aren't a symptom of an illness. Once this has been ruled out, you need to consider how to deal with your dog's altered

needs to make sure that their retirement is a happy and satisfactory experience for them.

Perhaps you notice while out on walks that your dog no longer trots ahead of you or pulls on the lead, but instead walks slowly and calmly next to or behind you. Dogs usually become somewhat more sedate in old age. They no longer move so quickly, and their reaction speed also slows down. This, however, has the inestimable advantage that it is possible to have more leisurely walks. It may be that a dog who once went chasing after every leaf now only gets moving for rabbits that pop up under its nose. A dog may now let all the other animals run free in order to enjoy the warm sun on its fur instead. It may be that your dog is just as tired after a short walk as they used to be after a long one, and disappears into their basket afterwards, not re-emerging for hours.

Your dog may now fail to react to you when you call them. Given that, as is the case with humans, hearing often becomes impaired in old age, your dog has probably not heard you. Maybe your dog also can't see as well as they once could, meaning that they fail even to notice you. Have no fear, though, even an older dog can learn to deal with new conditions. With your help your dog can achieve a new communication routine which is different and unfamiliar but which, as experience shows, will work just fine.

When you stroke your dog, you may feel a lump on or under their skin. Please do not fly into a panic straight away, as the formation of soft growths on the body is common in older dogs. In most cases these growths are benign and therefore don't necessarily require an operation. However, please keep an eye out for any

Older dogs may not be quite so quick on walks any more, but they are usually loyal and calm companions. (Photo:Tierfotoagentur/ Fischer)

changes in these lumps, and have them checked by your vet on a regular basis.

The familiar behaviour of your dog can also change when they get older. Your dog may entirely cast off their old fears, but it may also happen that the dog suddenly becomes scared of things that they used to face up to courageously. This different way of reacting may be linked with the dog's altered sensory perception, but other reasons may also be behind it.

Not necessarily a problem, but often extremely touching, is the need of many older dogs to be as close to their human as possible, and as often as possible. Allow your dog this closeness and grant the senior citizen privileges that you may not have permitted before. What objection can there be to treating the elderly gentleman or lady to a warm spot on the sofa, laying a sheepskin under the desk, or taking a snug basket with you to the office?

In this way the dog can be with you; with the composure that befits their old age, they will probably not be a disturbance but simply a quiet presence.

Your dog's ageing is not a process that will take place overnight, either. Have some consideration for the small changes that occur and gradually move away from habits when you sense that these are no longer doing your dog any good. The canine senior, with their altered needs, will help you to take the odd break in what is – after all – our often too hectic everyday life.

For example, you may have to stop your jogs through the woods together and find that you prefer to sit on a bench and enjoy the evening sun instead. This type of quiet companionship often brightens up life for both human and dog.

Characteristics of growing old: what changes at retirement age?

An elderly dog's body changes as time passes and, depending on their breed, signs of wear and tear will occur that the dog owner should deal with particularly carefully. If a dog is not in pain, they can often continue to join in with many things in extreme old age that they used to enjoy doing when young. Nevertheless it is important, particularly in old age, to observe the dog on an everyday basis to make sure that they are not placed under too much strain. An older dog that jumps into the car as happily as they ever did should be allowed to continue to do so. If, however, your dog waits for somebody to lift them in, this may be a sign that they are no longer able to jump into the car. In this case, a ramp designed for dogs will give relief for the owner's back. Additionally, it will spare the dog from trying to make potentially painful leaps into and out of the car.

Physical changes

 Mobility

I have already mentioned the older dog's restricted mobility, but here, too, there are immense differences, depending on breed and individual constitution. I know some dogs that are exceptions to the rule: a little Jack Russell, for example, who exceeded the fifteen-year mark long ago and still hops around his family like a bouncing ball. He flits about like a young dog and ends up sitting on the table just as fast as on the likewise rath-er elderly family pony. This certainly has something to do with the fact

The ramp is a relief for both dog and owner.
(Photo: JBTierfoto)

that he is a small dog who has always been very active. Although the musculature breaks down in older dogs, sufficient exercise slows down this process considerably. Many factors are mutually dependent here: as a result of a more porous bone structure in older dogs and a measurably thinner layer of cartilage in the joints, a dog may move less because this causes pain, or because they are stiff and are simply no longer able to execute a movement so well. Very large dogs can experience problems with the locomotor system even in their early years and, as old dogs, are often more placid and less mobile than small dogs.

Eyesight

Eyes are extremely sensitive sensory organs that can exhibit very different symptoms of disease. Pronounced sensitivity to light, blinking or winking, and redness in the eyes may be important clues to ocular diseases that must be taken seriously. Changed behaviour in the dog may also be attributable to visual impairment. Unusual fearfulness, snapping or even biting on sudden contact, and obvious uncertainty in unfamiliar locations (the dog may bump into furniture or objects that they are unable to see clearly) are signs that demand veterinary investigation.

If you look into an old dog's eyes, you can often see a clouding of the lens or the cornea that makes the eye look entirely different to that of a young dog. This clouding does not necessarily have to restrict the dog's eyesight. If, however, one of the ocular diseases that are familiar to humans, such as cataracts or glaucoma, is present, it can lead to blindness. In the chapter on diseases of the elderly dog you will learn more about these diseases, and how to handle and communicate with a dog that has poor vision or can no longer see at all.

 Hearing

As with restrictions in eyesight, deterioration in a dog's hearing can become noticeable through symptoms that are not obviously associated with a hearing problem. If the dog has trouble balancing, shows a change in their sleeping pattern, or stops reacting to well-known sounds, their ability to hear needs to be investigated in addition to a thorough general check-up.

Is somebody calling me? Even though this elderly dog is no longer able to hear and see so well, he still loves digging away! (Photo: Schmidt-Röger)

One day, one of the first dogs that grew old under my care stopped reacting the way he used to do when I called him. It was a while before I discovered that his hearing had failed considerably. For example, he stopped coming when I clattered about with food bowls and called him for dinner, something which he'd always been happy to interrupt any nap for. When I went to him and talked to him, I sometimes thought I saw him show something like fright, because he'd not heard me coming. From that point onwards I went up to him carefully, took the bowl with its delightful smell with me and calmly called the senior citizen to the table. Hearing declines in almost all dogs in old age, as the sensory hairs in the inner ear become less numerous. However, there are also diseases that can lead to total deafness in the dog. There will be more about this subject in the chapter on diseases.

 Metabolism

The absorption, conversion and breakdown of substances in the body all slow down in old age. This is influenced by the altered efficiency of the digestive tract, the condition of the major organs and teeth, and by hormone levels.

Reduced efficiency can have the effect that nutrients are no longer processed sufficiently well. The dog's energy requirement declines and they may react more sensitively to changes in food or feeding

Even spots can change in old age: in the case of the Dalmatian Dido, black and white remained clearly defined on his rump and tail right until the end; the spots faded on his face only, as can be seen in this photo. (Photo: Dr Schewior-Roland)

habits. This process of change can be tackled appropriately with an adapted feeding schedule and the right food.

 Fur

In addition to the tendency of the fur to go grey – which depends on the original colour, and does not only occur on the muzzle – the structure of the fur also changes as the dog grows older. The fur of an elderly dog requires a different kind of care, and the skin underneath needs to be examined regularly for changes, swellings or tissue alterations.

In the section on skin and fur care you will learn how this is done and how you can positively influence the condition of the fur from the inside too.

Behavioural changes

 Fearfulness

In old age, some dogs suddenly start to react differently to familiar things. There are dogs that react more nervously to sounds, movements or new surroundings than they ever did before, but also dogs that suddenly approach things they used to be really scared of in a much more laid-back way. Both cases can have many different causes.

The reduced ability to hear and see, but also degenerative processes in the dog's brain, may play a role here. There are dogs that actually do become more forgetful; they get lost even at home and we hardly recognise them in unfamiliar surroundings. It has been established that the symptoms of dementia as we know them in humans can also occur in dogs.

Once you have found out what's frightening your dog, you can learn to deal with the situation together. Do not deliberately expose the dog to this fear, but don't show excessive pity either, so that your dog doesn't feel that this behaviour is approved of. Try to gain the dog's trust and, if there are things that can't be avoided, show them that there is no need to be scared by, for example, striding courageously on ahead.

In most cases, fear of thunderstorms or fireworks can be allayed by not leaving the dog on their own at these times, and by heading together to a room where there is less exposure to the noise. Use the same rule here: do not talk to your dog sympathetically, but preferably do something nice with them instead: a game, a dog massage or a tickling session on the sofa accompanied by relaxing music.

Once the dog senses that you are laid-back and relaxed, they will be less scared and may even be able to overcome their fear.

 Barking

Barking is as inherent to dogs as mooing is to cows. The barking behaviour of dogs always has a reason but it can, unfortunately, also become self-perpetuating. Given that dogs learn by association, if a dog has on one occasion achieved success with a long round of barking – they received attention, for example somebody opened a door for them or kept them company – the dog will probably try to achieve the same result in a similar situation by barking again.

After this, the barking may progress to such a stage that it's no longer any use trying to ignore the dog. If this is the case, your dog needs to learn to form another association in this situation. This is where an experienced dog trainer is

Sometimes elderly dogs bark for no apparent reason. (Photo: Tierfotoagentur/ Schwerdtfeger)

best placed to help you: they can show you how you can regain control over your dog's barking behaviour.

Dogs whose thought processes are slower and who are already very old sometimes exhibit increased barking for no apparent reason. They commonly bark in situations where they're obviously lost and confused: this can be a spell in an unknown room, when they are at a distance from their pack (your family), or with an alternative daily routine they are not used to. If this is so, we as dog owners should take action by changing the situation.

In most cases all we need to do is encourage the dog to come over to us, offer them something familiar (basket, toy, chewy bone) and distract them for a little while so that they 'forget' the barking.

 Loner or clinger?

Being noticeably withdrawn – or alternatively tending not to want to leave their human alone at all – can be changes in behaviour shown by older dogs. If an erstwhile party animal suddenly prefers to hide away somewhere, this doesn't have to be an alarm signal. Have the dog checked to make sure that they are not coming down with any illness. If everything is in order healthwise, you should simply let the dog be. We cannot oblige them to keep us company. Perhaps the dog needs some peace, and we should respect that.

Older dogs sometimes react to their fellow canines in a different way from that shown in their younger years.

(Photo: Tierfotoagentur/ Richter)

Incontinence

Your hitherto house-trained dog may start leaving behind little puddles in the house, even though you take them for walks regularly. You can assume that the dog has not suddenly unlearned their house training, and that there is no malicious intent behind it either. Punishment would therefore be totally inappropriate. Incontinence in old age can have various causes, and I will go into these in closer detail in the chapter on illnesses in canine old age.

 Sleeping

An older dog gets tired sooner, and may stop leaping out of their basket for the second extended stroll of the day but remain snugly tucked up. In the mornings, especially, our elderly mongrel bitch loves a lie-in in her basket or on the bed and can't be persuaded to leave the house to do her necessary business until the late morning. Elderly dogs sleep considerably more and for longer periods than dogs in mid-life do. The most important thing, then, is an undisturbed spot, out of the way of draughts but from which the old dog can still keep enough of an eye on life around them.

Character changes

If you get the impression that your dog is changing to such an extent that you barely know them, you simply must get to the bottom of it. Aggressive behaviour on encountering fellow canines which was never seen before, and for no apparent reason, unsettledness and nervousness in a usually laid-back character, or previously unheard-of shyness can, just like limitless confidence, be signs of a pathological process. This is also the case for unwonted detachment in a dog that used to love being in the thick of things. Degenerative diseases of the brain, but also infectious diseases, may be the cause here.

Why it is so wonderful to have an old dog

Anyone who takes the time to get to know their old dog all over again will notice that life together takes on a new dimension.

Your dog has changed; they have perhaps become more unhurried, more sedate, and more grizzled. This is the very time when we can learn a lot from our elderly canine companions. Our everyday life is often extremely fast-paced; there is sometimes little time really to enjoy the small things in life. An older dog may make us pause occasionally, and we can look into the eyes of our dog and remember our years together and the experiences that have changed not only our dog. Even if it's not always easy to care for an older dog, there are so many wonderful things in a life with an elderly dog that I can only urge you to enjoy this time as intensively as possible.

The autumn of life: worldly-wise and well-mannered

You no doubt devoted a lot of time to bringing up your young dog and may have despaired when the dog failed to do what they should be doing. Perhaps they pulled on the lead, did their own thing on walks, or regularly went on the rampage when they encountered other dogs. Even though dogs generally don't shed their characteristics completely in old age, in most cases they will be more laid-back overall. Many old dogs that needed to be put on the lead in various situations when they were younger have now become so attached to their owners that they'll follow them faithfully, no matter what happens.

With a young dog, you need to keep a constant eye out for mischief. The dog steals the cake from the table before you can blink, shreds the third new dog basket just when you were thinking this phase had passed, and goes into overdrive when the postman comes. In most cases older dogs, in contrast, have learned what they are allowed to do, and what is forbid-

Child and dog: this elderly Dalmatian is acting as assistant baby-sitter here. This is only appropriate when adults are close by and the dog is thoroughly dependable.

(Photo: Dr Schewior-Roland)

den. They may also be simply too tired or too stiff to jump on to the chair and then on to the table, or are no longer able to hear when somebody is at the door.

If the old dog does not suffer from incontinence, doing their business becomes a simpler affair than it is with a young dog. Although some older dogs may need to go out more often, they are not necessarily tied to fixed times. In most cases they will indicate clearly when they want to go out, do their business quickly, and then head off back to their basket and disappear under their warm blanket.

To communicate with your old dog, very few words or even just a look are often sufficient. The dog has been a family member for years, and found their place in the pack long ago. This makes companionship more stress-free and more of a matter of routine.

Friends for life: the old dog and their human

For the human, spending ten, fourteen or even sixteen years with a dog means that a lot has happened during this time. Maybe you've built a house, moved house, brought up children and experienced

Even when you acquire a dog that is already elderly, it is possible to build up a deep relationship.

(Photo: Tierfotoagentur/ Schwerdtfeger)

other things that your old dog has been through with you. Your dog has absorbed your moods just as much as they have noticed changes in the family pack or the move to a new home. These experiences have shaped your dog, too, and during this time they have probably become even more attached to you than they were in younger years. Maybe you're noticing that your dog is now trying to be where you are much more often than they did before. An elderly dog is often content with very little and is glad to be in a warm spot close to their human, from where they can look

out and observe what's going on around them. When your dog cuddles in a little closer on the sofa, suddenly lays their head on your knee under the desk, or throws you a glance that goes straight to your heart, the fondness that has been developing between you over many years is tangible.

It is wonderful to regard the encounter with this elderly dog as a friendship and to accept the gifts that such an alliance brings with it. For you, this may mean meeting the dog and their needs halfway and adapting yourself to their new, slower pace. Once you have sensed the positive effects this calmness and reflection can have, you will be sure to appreciate the deep bond with your dog even more.

Slowing down: discovering leisure

Even if your dog was a lightning-quick hunter in former times, they may now only raise their head briefly when a rabbit shoots out of a bush during a walk. The senior dog not only sees the rabbit later, it also appears not to be as important to them as it used to be, perhaps because they have already seen and chased many rabbits during their lifetime. This has the inestimable advantage that even former hunters need not necessarily be kept on the lead during their walks. They often trot alongside us at an unhurried pace, sniff here and there, and are happy with a brief tour. Sometimes they potter along behind us and no longer keep up their customary walking pace.

We have to stop again and again and wait for them. Dragging an old dog behind you or otherwise forcing them to move faster would be downright cruel. Perhaps your dog wants to run faster to make sure they don't lose you, but they

may be unable to do so anymore because their bones and muscles are no longer co-operating. In this case it's great if we can learn to slow down and make our walks less hurried. What objection can there be to taking a break on a bench, looking at a picturesque view, and reflecting on your life? We should reduce our walking pace, breathe more evenly and pause once in a while. In this way, we also achieve the calmness that our old dog shows with their slow pace.

Here's looking at you: dignified old age

Looking into an old dog's eyes frequently moves me to tears. Often, it is more than the fleeting glance of a young dog, who looks only to check that their human is still there. Old dogs gaze longer and more profoundly, and sometimes we are reflected in the cloudy eyes of our old friend. With one look into an old dog's eyes, the certainty that life together isn't going to last for ever becomes just as clear as the proverbial faithfulness that has grown over the years. I find that older dogs have a particular kind of dignity in old age, which is reflected in their eyes.

To me, even though a dog is a dog, this look contains something extremely wise and knowing. It impresses me again and again, and I believe that our dogs actually do know much more than we think.

Faithful companion: the old dog in everyday life

Because your older dog has become so easygoing and appreciates your company in a new and special way, you can and should include the elderly dog even more in your everyday life. If they indicate that they'd like to join in, you should consider whether it's possible to have the dog accompany you. I know an occupational therapist who takes her old labrador with her on all home visits. Although this dog is not a trained therapy dog, he delights the patients with his quiet presence and visibly enjoys being there. The attention a dog receives when they accompany us on such simple errands as a visit to the hairdresser, or a shopping trip for dog food, does their soul good and gives them the feeling that they really belong and are part of their human's life. Do not hide your old dog away.

On the contrary, put them on a special pedestal during the autumn and winter of their life. Take particularly good care of your senior dog: honour them with a particularly chic collar, visit their favourite places just with them, and feel free to show them favouritism if you have a number of dogs. Of course, the old dog must be neither pampered nor anthropomorphised. Nevertheless, you should show them how much you love them; your companion will return this love in their own way. A close coexistence will give rise to many wonderful memories that will be sure to comfort you when your friend is no longer with you.

Healthy and fit during the best years of their life

Older dogs don't have to either smell bad or have shaggy fur. Their eyes can shine like those of a young dog, and their nails should be carefully maintained at a suitable length. However, things that can be taken for granted in many young dogs often require more intensive attention in older dogs. In addition to correct grooming, diet plays an important role, which is why there is a section devoted specifically to this topic later in the book.

There are many opportunities to keep old dogs physically and mentally fit without asking too much of them. This way of

interacting with dogs is fun and brightens up life for both dog and human. Additional comforts in the senior canine's everyday life alleviate the difficulties that old age can bring with it. The topic of wellness for older dogs should receive more attention, to make sure that dogs of advanced years can be helped to feel completely contented.

Grooming an older dog

Grooming an old dog correctly is no more difficult than it is with a young dog. On the contrary, the older animal usually knows what's going on, trusts their human and stays still because they enjoy the special attention. Getting hold of the right tools does make sense if you don't have dental and nail care performed by the vet or groomer.

Once you've got the equipment at home, you'll also be able to use them for your younger dogs and possibly for the next-door neigh-bour's pets. Take time to care for your dog and turn them into the most important family member while doing so. Go on, treat them to something nice, even if their life doesn't depend on it: a special dog shampoo maybe, a touch of spray to make their fur shine, or a massage using a little olive oil. Finally, dress them in their Sunday-best collar and tell them how great they look. I promise you, they'll be delighted! The walk afterwards will be fun and relaxing for dog and human – good for the soul, so to speak.

Skin and fur care

Nutrition is skin care from the inside and therefore takes top priority. Nevertheless, depending on their hair length, you will need to take special care of your dog's fur as well when they grow older. The fur often becomes drier and more brittle and, in some dogs, becomes matted more quickly than it used to in their younger years. For breeds that need to be trimmed, the services of an experienced dog groomer must not be skimped on. The groomer will be able to estimate the characteristics of the fur accurately, even in an old dog, and will know how to deal with them correctly. If you have 'plucked' your dog yourself up to now, of course you can continue to do so. However, please keep an eye on the way the undercoat develops.

In some dogs, hair growth declines in old age and the plucking suddenly begins to hurt them. Have a skin disease ruled out by your vet and discuss an alternative grooming option with the dog groomer. In this case, professional shearing may be the solution, and this can also help dogs with longer fur if the hair becomes matted too quickly. Dogs with longer fur (rough collies, for example) need to be brushed thoroughly at least every other day.

Take a look at parts with a lot of hair often enough to make sure that there are no matted nests forming that will provide potential parasites with a wonderful living environment. If badly matted clumps of hair do form, you can try to cut them out very carefully with blunt-ended scissors. However, do not under any circumstances injure the skin, which is often very thin in these places; it is generally best to seek help from the groomer or vet, especially if your dog is likely to wriggle.

Short-haired dogs don't require much more skin care in old age than they did when they were younger. However, a regular warm bath with a natural soap for dogs that is effective against fleas and ticks does them good. Afterwards, rub your dog dry down and stay indoors with them until their fur is thoroughly dry. Some dogs like to be wrapped in a big bath towel, and will even stay lying in it or under it after they are dry. Special dog handtowels, which are especially absorbent, are also available.

Dental care

If you've never cleaned your dog's teeth before, now is the time to start doing it, preferably after a thorough cleaning and dental examination at the vet's. Regular tooth care will prevent the formation of plaque and subsequent tartar, which attacks the substance of the teeth.

Don't ambush your dog with the toothbrush, and don't bend over them either if you can avoid it. You can make a start by slipping a gauze fingerstall from the chemist over your finger and then adding a little water and special dog toothpaste to it. Rub carefully over the teeth and watch how your dog behaves. If it's an easy task, you can introduce a dog toothbrush featuring a double arrangement of bristles to clean the teeth inside and out. If the dog struggles, though, it makes sense to leave the regular dental care to your vet, who should be checking your pet's teeth every six months in any case.

A powder called Plaque Off®, which is strongly scented with algae, can be administered via the dog's food. It is said

Tooth cleaning is called for!

You're reading correctly! Not only should humans clean their teeth regularly, but there's no getting past dental care for our four-legged friends, either. Three times a day would be overdoing it, but three times a week, especially for the older dog, is appropriate. Please do not under any circumstances use a toothpaste that is intended for humans. The foam that's produced can lead to stomach problems in your dog and some of the components may be toxic to them. There are special dog toothpastes that have a taste that appeals to dogs. The tooth-paste can be applied using a special dog toothbrush (available in pet shops or from your vet) or a finger toothbrush. The outer surfaces of the teeth are particularly important in this process, as the dog's tongue largely cleans the inside surfaces. It is therefore not necessary for the dog to open their mouth wide during teeth cleaning; you only need to lift the cheeks a little. 'Pretreatment' using a mouth spray for dogs will help to shift stubborn tooth deposits. There are also chewy bones that partially assume the function of a toothbrush. They commonly contain chlorophyll, which counters bad breath. Offer your dog these bones as a supplement to their regular teeth cleaning.

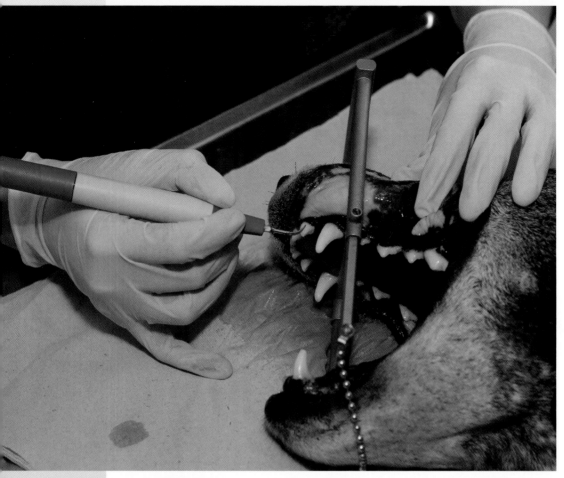

Although it looks as though it takes a bit of getting used to, the dog notices nothing of professional dental cleaning. A sedative or anaesthetic administered by the vet leaves the dog to dream during the treatment.

(Photo: JBTierfoto)

to prevent tartar formation and the unpleasant breath associated with it. The product originates in Sweden and the address of the supplier is at the end of the book.

Some types of chewy bone provide good supplementary dental care for the dog. Bear in mind that your older dog may no longer be able and willing to chew such big and hard bones as they used to. A chewy shoe made from thin cow's hide or special chewy materials for dental care are still attractive to most old dogs, and your dog will retreat contentedly to their basket with a treat of this type.

Ear care

Dogs of all ages can get ear problems, which is why regular check-ups and cleaning of the ears are important, not only for the older dog. However, an undetected and therefore untreated disease of the ears may lead to permanent damage, which may not become noticeable until the dog's old age. Clean your dog's ears regularly using cleaning cloths intended for the purpose or a small wad of cotton wool (never with cotton buds), or leave this to the vet or dog groomer. Alarm signals for ear problems are a bad smell, frequent ear

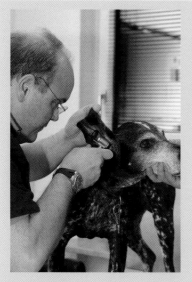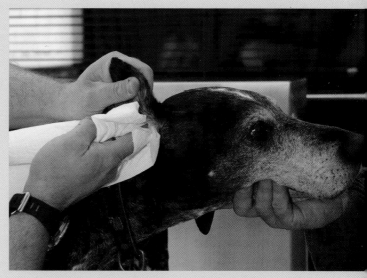

Thorough examination and cleaning of the senior dog's ears should be a matter of course during the regular check-up by your vet. (Photo: JBTierfoto)

scratching, flinching on contact, discharge from the ear, and potentially difficulties with balancing.

Paw and nail care

Depending on the shape of your dog's paws, and the surfaces on which they regularly walk, the nails may wear down without it being necessary to cut them on

When cutting a dog's nails you must be careful not to cut too near the quick. It is best to allow a professional to perform this important task.

(Photo: JBTierfoto)

a regular basis. However, because the older dog may be joining you on long walks less often and will be exercising somewhat less overall, it is possible that their nails will need to be cut more often, especially if they seldom making contact with the ground when the dog walks. If the nails are light coloured it is possible to recognise the part with the blood supply (the 'quick') easily and to cut off only the transparent tip of the nail using special clippers. Your vet or dog groomer should perform the trimming of dark-coloured nails. If you do happen to cut too deep, though, there's no need to fly into a panic. Staunch the bleeding using alum (e.g. a styptic pencil), or press a handkerchief on to the bleeding nail until the bleeding stops by itself.

Older dogs sometimes have dry and cracked paws, especially in the winter. To help with this problem you can buy greasy ointments in specialist stores that you can rub into the balls of the paw before a walk in the snow or rain.

Fitness training: how canine seniors stay mobile

It will do your older dog good if you can give them the exercise that they need. It is great for both of you if this is not always the same old stroll around the block. Varied walks with brief games in between strolls will delight even the older dog. If your dog is able to turn the walk into an adventure, encounter one or two canine colleagues, or is even able still to be active in canine sports (as far as their capabilities will allow), they will probably also remain mentally fit for a good while longer. The

rule here is to avoid asking too little, but also to avoid asking too much.

A rolling stone gathers no moss

Nobody knows your dog as well as you, unless perhaps you didn't adopt your dog until they'd already reached canine old age. Was your dog always one of those who, after a long walk, suddenly popped up in front of you with a ball, wanting to get active again? Or were they, even in younger years, a rather more sedate customer, who would head straight for their basket even after a quick stroll? Try to find out what your dog still can and still wants to do. Keep a close eye on them in this context too. Do they run along happily with you, or do they soon start lagging behind? Could your dog perhaps be in pain, or is it only the monotony of the never-changing route?

Regular exercise keeps your dog fit; nevertheless, a dog should never be forced to do anything that they don't want to do (any more) or are unable to do (any more). Adjust walks and exercise opportunities to your dog's capabilities. Go on three short walks rather than a really long one. During these walks, integrate active games for your senior dog that also challenge them mentally. Even older dogs are often still able to jump over a tree trunk, run along the top of a low wall or clamber up a small hill. Tracks laid down with treats, slalom courses in the woods, or hidden dummies turn walks with older dogs into a particular pleasure.

If your dog has always enjoyed running alongside your bicycle, they can continue to do this in old age if this poses no difficulties for them. It's the same rule here: if the dog runs along briskly, it's clearly fun for them; if, however, they drag along behind or even start to hobble, you should put your bicycle in the shed straight away. Because

Shared bicycle trips are fun.

When the old dog gets tired, he makes himself comfortable in the bicycle trailer. (Photos: JBTierfoto)

older dogs are no longer able to run such long distances, a special bicycle trailer for dogs can provide relief. Ensure that the dog is sitting comfortably inside and is not exposed to any draughts.

Adventures with older dogs

Even in old age, most dogs enjoy making an experience out of things and accompa-

nying their human in everyday life. A bicycle or car trip is a welcome change for the older dog. If you often used to take your dog with you, there is no argument in favour of leaving the old dog at home now. As old dogs are often calmer, sometimes it is even easier to take the dog with you to work, to the golf course or to the pub. Given that an elderly dog no longer enjoys lying down on cold, hard floors quite so

Hydrotherapy provides support during rehabilitation following illnesses, and helps to build up fitness again.

(Photo: animals-digital/Brodmann/Kynofit)

much, it is advisable to take along a blanket that can be rolled up and put in your bag. When you take your companion into town with you, please consider that the noise, sights and smells may be too much for the elderly dog. This also applies to events that you may have considered taking your dog to in the past. Whereas they used to go with you to the market, the dog show or the game fair, they may now find it difficult to process the many impressions and noises found there. If you embark upon adventures with your dog, then please make absolutely sure that they are able to lie down and have a rest in a cool and shady spot every now and then.

Fitness

Even an old dog can rebuild fitness following a period of rest, which may have been enforced by illness or convalescence – although of course, as with humans, this will not occur overnight. It does nobody any good to rest for the whole week and then embark upon a forced march for three hours at the weekend. It's the same rule here: build the dog's strength up slowly so that they can achieve fitness. Increase the daily walk or bicycle trip by one more short section every other day, or integrate active games with your dog along the way – games which you can then expand on.

In this context, too, keep a close eye on your dog in order to avoid asking too much of them. Everything that they join in with happily is probably fun for them; if you notice that their energy is dwindling, it's best to reduce the workload a little.

Swimming builds up fitness, too. Specially trained dog physiotherapists offer supervised hydrotherapy sessions for dogs who need to build up fitness in a specific manner, are suffering from a disorder of the locomotor system (in this case, swimming serves as a rehabilitation measure following treatment or an operation), or dogs with neurological disorders.

Canine sports with older dogs

Dogs that enjoyed canine sports with their owners in their younger years shouldn't be retired from service because they may not be winning contests anymore. Nevertheless, there are age restrictions, which are intended to help avoid placing older dogs under too much strain.

In most cases, the cut-off age is nine or ten years at the most; depending on performance and the conditions under which they are kept, hunting dogs are deemed to be seniors from the age of eight to nine years. However, if you have your dog undergo an annual health check-up at the vet's from the age of eight, you will still be able to allow your dog (as long as they are healthy, and working within their capabilities) to join in at training sessions even if, due to their age, they are no longer allowed to take part in competitions.

It is also mandatory to have a blood test performed at the vet's. Potential signs of illness existing in the blood can be detected early, before physical symptoms arise. You will then be able to provide the appropriate treatment more swiftly and get your senior sports-dog fit again.

Mental training for canine seniors

Keeping older dogs mentally fit is enormous fun! It is so wonderful to see how your elderly companion livens up when given tricky tasks every now and again, or when they are taught something new. And you're wide of the mark if you think that old dogs can't learn new tricks! Many a canine senior still has great fun learning tricks or searching for a dummy in the woods.

These tricks should, of course, be easy to perform for the older dog. This is where tricks that call on wits but where mobility doesn't play such a big part are ideal. Dogs who have learned to pick up and carry something in their mouths on command can, for example, carry a bag of food home from the shop, or a newspaper. You won't believe how proud an older dog can be to receive a task like this. They will perform it conscientiously!

Tricks can be practical, too: the old dog has something to keep him busy, and you don't have to carry your shopping yourself!

(Photo: JBTierfoto)

Ideas for fun and games

 Tidying up

Do you have a junior dog in the house that leaves everything lying around? Teach your senior dog to tidy the stuff up. For this purpose, the younger dog needs to be sent off into another room or on a walk for the time being so that they won't thwart the plans. Teach your older dog how to pick up the toys if they don't already know how to. Place a small laundry basket or cardboard box in the middle of the room. To start with, put a toy into the dog's mouth and give the request 'Hold' or 'Take'.

As soon as the dog gets near the box, reward this action with a clicker or treat. Nudge the box so that the dog automatically drops the toy into it in order to receive the reward. Just before they drop it, say 'In the basket', or 'Tidy up!'. Dogs who are familiar with retrieval learn this game really fast. However, a dog who has never enjoyed having something in its mouth will perhaps have more fun during the next game.

 Opening a pedal bin

The question is, of course, whether this is what you want: dogs that open the pedal bin can also help themselves from it when you are not there. Perhaps you should simply surprise your senior with his own pedal bin. The dog will learn to step on to the pedal of the bin on the command 'Touch'. They will learn this by means of step-by-step affirmation and reward. The individual elements – touching the pedal, stepping on to the pedal and thereby opening the lid, letting go of the pedal and thereby closing the lid – can be taught, for example, with the aid of a clicker or a

treat. If your dog also has the knack of tidying up, these two games can be combined wonderfully.

> You will find more tricks of this kind in **Trick School for Dogs** by Manuela Zaitz, Cadmos 2008
> (ISBN 978-3-86127-960-0)

 Tracking

Even old dogs can search for tracks that you lay out for them, using treats for example, at home, in the garden, in an open space or in the woods. In the process, place less importance on perfection than on the fun you will have together. If your dog's nose is no longer so efficient, lay a track that has a strong smell, using bits of tripe or fish treats, for example. If your dog is no longer able to use their eyes effectively, choose clearly visible treats so that they have a chance of finding them.

For dogs who are familiar with searching for tracks, you can also drag a trail (by dragging something that smells delicious across the ground) and allow the dog to search afterwards. A particularly fun game is searching for small scented tubes filled with something strong smelling. It is possible to make these at home, but a durable and tested version of these so-called 'sniffers' can now be ordered from specialist stores (see Internet addresses at the end of the book). The advantage of these is that the dog is able to see and smell the treats easily – ideal for older dogs.

 Find-the-treat

Take a number of containers made from cardboard, plastic or tin (be careful, no sharp edges allowed), and hide treats or something else your dog loves beneath

Older dogs love warmth and can even learn to cover themselves up.

(Photo: animals-digital/Brodmann)

them. To begin with, show your dog that you are hiding something beneath the containers. The rewarding of individual steps applies here, too: initially, the dog's action is affirmed and they are rewarded just for approaching the container.

After a few repetitions, you should reward only when your dog touches a container with their nose. Finally, the dog will receive the reward automatically once they have tapped the container with their nose to make it fall over. To begin with, help out a little so that your senior dog experiences success and doesn't lose interest. Every time you give a reward, don't forget

to deduct the treats from the daily food ration so that your dog doesn't run to unnecessary fat.

 Covering up

Given that older dogs are fonder of warmth than young dogs who are constantly on the move, it makes sense to teach the senior to cover themselves up. The best way to start is by having the dog lie down and laying a blanket across their back. With the request 'Hold' or 'Take', or another command that the dog associates with holding, the tip of the blanket is placed into the dog's mouth so that they continue to cover themselves automatically.

As soon as the dog shows the desired behaviour, they are rewarded with a clicker or a treat, and an appropriate phrase, such as 'Sleep tight', is introduced. The more successfully this task goes, the later (i.e. once the dog is really covered up) the dog is rewarded. Thus, your dog will be able to learn, step by step, what is expected of them.

Support for old bones

Even if your dog used to lie down everywhere or take a long running leap into the car, keep an eye out for the moment when either activity becomes more difficult. Your dog may now only rarely lie down if there is no soft place for lying down nearby (or allowed), or may get up with a struggle when they've been lying on a cold floor. Stop expecting this of the senior. Old dogs deserve to have even better care taken of them than previously may have been the case. A soft spot for lying down in is part of the package, just like a ramp for the car (or a strong arm) and, for short-haired dogs, a warm blanket or even a coat or raincoat.

Climbing aids and stair gates

The aids that you can offer your older dog can be adapted according to the obstacles they need to overcome in everyday life. Does your dog suddenly come to a stop at the back of the car, no longer jumping in like a rubber ball? If you have a small dog, you can lift them carefully into the car, where of course a soft blanket or a well-

cushioned travel basket will be waiting for them. Bigger dogs can receive support in the form of specially designed climbing aids. Whether this is a small extendable ramp fitted in the car, or a bridge set up against it, your dog will thus be able to overcome the height difference with ease. This preserves joints, sinews, ligaments and old bones, and prevents injuries.

Do not allow your dog to climb stairs unnecessarily, either. If your dog is small enough for you to be able to carry them up easily, don't forget that they'll have to come down again. If their eyesight is poor and they are no longer so steady on their feet, it is advisable to install a stair gate at the top and bottom of the stairs. The dog will then be able to climb the stairs only with your help, and the risk that they'll fall down them is reduced. Just don't make your dog wait too long at the top or the bottom.

Large dogs may have been living downstairs already, and it doesn't bother them when the rest of the pack disappears upstairs at night. If your big dog has always come upstairs with you, though, don't suddenly leave them downstairs alone. Either join forces to carry them up at night and back down again in the morning, relocate your bedroom to the lower reaches of the house, or take the decision to provide them with a doggy friend who can join them in guarding the downstairs area.

Soft spots for lying in

During their younger years, many dogs enjoy lying on cool tiles in the kitchen and will even sleep on concrete slabs on the terrace. The older they get, the more arduous this becomes, especially if they've been lying in one spot for a while. Cold, damp,

Resi had arthritis and wore a coat and warm sleeves not because it looked attractive, but because she needed the warmth, especially in the snow. She lived to the grand old age of 18 years and 5 months.

(Photo: Kamp)

but also hard floors bother them more than they used to, and they'll even avoid lying down if there is no pleasant spot available for doing so. However, you have the dilemma that, on the one hand, they'd love to go with you everywhere, but on the other hand, you don't always have a soft blanket available. You can rectify this situation. There are wonderful, wash-able mats with a non-slip underside, which originate from human medicine and are actually designed to provide elderly people with a soft, pressure-free place to lie down; they are therefore ideal for your old dog.

The mats can be ordered in large sizes and cut into pieces that are just right for the dog. These mats can be placed everywhere that your dog enjoys spending time, in addition to their customary and long-established spots. As takeaway options there are even fleece blankets that can be rolled up and draped. A mat folded up in the backpack also does the job on excursions.

Warm blankets, cosy coats

Dogs in coats often prompt a patronising smile. Rightly so, in some cases: if a dog

with normal fur is encased in shiny little PVC coat in average weather conditions, this is not appropriate to the animal's needs. However, if it is raining hard or if the temperature drops to freezing point or below, for many elderly dogs a dog coat is no longer a superfluous luxury. Thin-skinned dogs, such as greyhounds and some other short-haired dogs, feel the cold more easily and could do with a second skin if they are no longer exercising so regularly owing to old age.

Some old dogs with arthritis or similar disorders will be helped by a warming coat, or even a pullover indoors during the day, if the weather is somewhat cooler. As

Wellness day for dog and human

Go on, spend a day just with you and your dog! This will not only advance your relationship, but may perhaps give you a short break from everyday life as well.

Start the day leisurely and slowly, enjoy the fact that your old dog is with you, and fuss them in all the places where they love to be touched. Watch them closely as you do so: when do they stretch languorously or relax completely?

Then go off for a walk at a particularly attractive location. Does your dog love the beach and the sea, or do they prefer bounding about in the woods? Does your dog enjoy a car journey? Turn the day trip into a treat for yourself as well and combine the journey with a relaxing lunch at a dog-friendly pub (don't forget the dog blanket).

Enjoy the day together and, in the process, reflect on all the things you have experienced with your four-legged companion so far. Adjust yourself to the pace of your old friend, and don't forget to schedule rest breaks during which the dog can sleep and you have time to let your thoughts wander.

Show your dog a little piece of the world that they haven't seen before, or go somewhere they have always enjoyed visiting. Observe your dog, play with them,

Australian shepherd Jake is eleven years old in this photo. He is visibly enjoying the day by the sea. His owner says: 'Day trips together have made our relationship even more intense.'

(Photo: Bosselmann)

or simply sit on a bench together and watch the world go by.

Take time to be there just for your dog, and spend the evening as well without bustle and stress. Massage your dog, if they like this; take a foot-bath yourself after the walk and make yourself a special cup of tea while your dog eats their favourite food.

You are both bound to sleep soundly and contentedly after such an intensive day together.

a result, the muscles remain warm and the dog is able to move about with greater ease. The important thing is that the jacket fits well, isn't pinching anywhere and enables the dog to do their business. For dogs that are sensitive to the cold, their basket should be as close as possible to a heat source that's pleasant for the dog. If this is not possible, the dog can be covered with a warm blanket. Many dogs are able to creep under the blanket easily by themselves and snuggle up so that they can barely be seen.

Wellness for older dogs

'Wellness' is a word on everyone's lips; why not for old dogs? In fact, wellness means nothing less than wellbeing. This is exactly what we desire, and not only for our old dog. There are many opportunities to do things with your dog during which both of you will feel thoroughly good in the process. Depending on the breed, there are different situations in which dogs feel particularly contented. For example, a husky loves a walk in the snow,

Golden retriever Bosse never goes in the water without a life-jacket now since he went under in the reeds and had to be rescued by the fire brigade. At his advanced age, he no longer had the strength to reach the bank.
(Photo: JBTierfoto)

while a Yorkshire terrier, due to their tiny size, will sink into it, get wet and probably feel less at ease. Therefore, don't ask anything of your dog which they have never enjoyed before.

Swimming

For dogs that enjoy swimming by nature, a dip in the favourite lake or a day at the seaside is a particularly wonderful experience. Swim with your dog and run along the shore to warm up again afterwards. Floating toys will also keep your dog happy. Dummies, which are small canvas toys used for retrieval work, usually float and are therefore particularly suitable. Please make sure that the water and the air temperature are not too cold and that your dog won't need to run about wet out of doors for too long. Dry your dog, but particularly an old dog, immediately after swimming if it doesn't happen to be high summer. Swimming takes up a lot of energy, and you should take care that the old dog doesn't over-exert itself out of sheer enthusiasm. Therefore, don't throw the dummy too often, and don't try to swim long distances in deep water with your dog; this could very soon become too much of a good thing for the dog's heart, lungs and muscles. When you are by the sea, you should always have fresh drinking water ready for your senior dog so that they don't start drinking salt water out of sheer thirst.

If this does happen, though, don't fly into a panic. In most cases, dogs will expel the water very quickly and be unharmed.

Bathing

There are dogs that love being bathed. They just stand in the bathtub and serenely allow themselves to be lathered up, showered down or even blow-dried.

However, many do not like it at all. Nevertheless, old dogs are precisely the ones that benefit from a bath now and then. They may not be cleaning themselves as thoroughly as they used to do and may also smell more 'doggy' than before. Special dog shampoos or soaps that simultaneously provide protection against ticks and fleas clean the dog's skin and fur thoroughly, but gently. A small squirt of baby oil in the water has a lipid-replenishing effect and protects against dryness. However, to ensure that the skin's hydrolipid film isn't destroyed and the protective layer of lipids remains intact, you must not bathe any dog too frequently.

Never force your dog to take a bath, but proceed extremely gently. If you have a good relationship, the dog will trust you when you lift them into the bathtub or shower. If your dog tries to escape, a calm

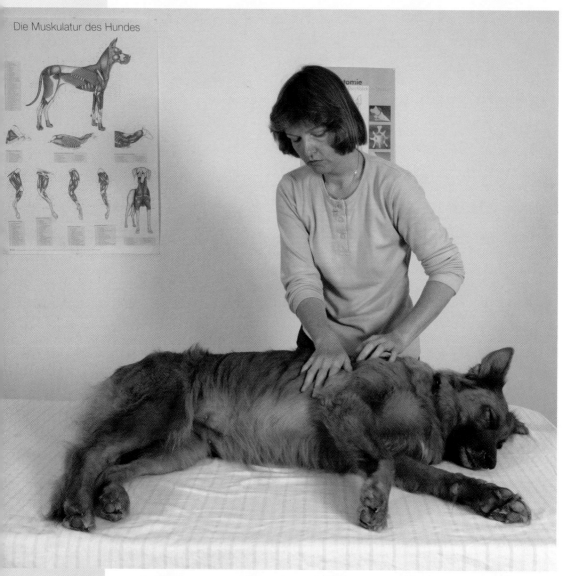

Die Muskulatur des Hundes

Professional massage is offered for dogs as well; this is indicated particularly after accidents or operations.

(Photo: animals-digital/Brodmann)

assistant can provide support. Feel free to reward the dog with a treat if they submit to the procedure placidly. Additionally, make sure that the water is a pleasant temperature and that no shampoo gets into the dog's eyes and mouth. Blow-drying is unnecessary; it is too loud and often much too hot. Rub the dog down thoroughly and leave them to dry in a warm place in peace. With long-haired dogs you should brush the damp fur carefully after a bath.

Massage

Massage promotes wellbeing – and is an experience that we humans greatly enjoy. There are now entire books devoted to the various forms of canine massage. Find out what your dog likes best! This could be a powerful massage using a special brush, a hedgehog massage ball or a massage glove. The calming Tellington-Touch®, which not only has a positive effect on the musculature and breathing but is also able to alleviate fears and pain, has also proven its worth in dogs.

Elderly dogs often suffer from muscle cramps, which can be extremely painful. The cause may be a disorder of the locomotor system (in this case it is mandatory to ask the vet first whether massage is appropriate), but also the cold or excessive strain.

To perform the massage, lay a blanket on the floor so that the dog can lie comfortably, and exclude all potential disruption. Start with gentle strokes and observe your dog's reactions. Never force them to stay lying down! Some dogs prefer to enjoy a massage while sitting or standing, and they may also relax visibly in the process.

The quiet zone

Both puppies and old dogs require a particularly large amount of rest. To ensure that they get it, you must make sure that a warm comfortable basket or dog bed is placed somewhere where the entire family isn't constantly trampling past. I therefore recommend installing at least two beds for the senior dog: one in a spot where they can take everything in if they want to be part of things, and the second in a spot to which they can retreat when they are tired of the bustle. Old dogs usually decide this for themselves. There came a point when one of my canine seniors was so fond of retreating that we had to take care not to shut him in anywhere. While we had visitors downstairs and children were playing, he would lie asleep under the covers in the bedroom. I even had to go and fetch him at dinner time, as he was no longer able to hear the food bowl clattering from that distance.

Cocker spaniel Lilly enjoys some peace and quiet in a particularly comfortable dog bed.

(Photo: Brockmann)

To him, the most important thing is that it's tasty.

(Photo:Tierfotoagentur/ Richter)

Meals on wheels or soft canned food:

How to feed an older dog correctly

Feeding dogs is a science in itself. Whole hosts of vets and other specialists are preoccupied with creating the ultimate food for dogs and offering food that's more and more specifically adapted to breeds and medical conditions. Although opinions are somewhat divided as to what type of food is the best, it is largely agreed that the needs of an older dog differ considerably from those of the younger dog, and the diet is no exception.

Home-cooked or bought?

If you've got the time and like the idea of cooking the senior dog's food yourself, you've found a new hobby! It's fun to busy yourself with buying and preparing the ingredients for a balanced diet; however, you must be able to schedule sufficient time for the purpose.

Essentially, it can be assumed that dog food in a wide variety of formulations contains what the dog needs in order to receive balanced nutrition. Doing your own cooking is therefore only effective if the home-prepared food is able to meet this requirement. Symptoms of dietary deficiency, which can be fatal for older dogs in particular, may be the consequence of an incomplete diet.

Dry food

Dry food has many advantages: it is easy to feed to the dog, easy to take with you on trips, and there are special formulations with components that are tuned to the nutritional needs of older dogs.

Basically, therefore, one can't go too far wrong with a good quality dry food for senior dogs. Nevertheless, it is also important to take a careful look at how the older dog is living their life: if they are still as happy as can be, racing around with their younger canine pals, they may need richer food than if they spend the whole day on the couch. For dogs that have become too fat due to illness, lack of exercise or incorrect feeding, high quality dietary food will be an aid to slimming (always discuss this with the vet!), in addition to the appropriate exercise.

If your dog's teeth have fallen out or worn down, or need to be extracted, it will of course be difficult for them to crunch dry food and thereby prepare it for digestion. Experiment to find out what your dog can eat easily, even with few teeth, or switch to good canned food after consulting with your vet.

Canned food

For dogs that can no longer chew correctly following dental treatment, canned food can be a solution. However, in this context, just as with other food prepara-tions, please look out for quality. Cheap is not always bad, and expensive is not always good. Become informed about dog food tests and, if possible, pick a food that's performed very well in the ratings. There are now premium canned foods that can be fed to dogs who are no longer able to ingest other food formulations effectively.

Especially when feeding canned food, though, keep a close eye on the dog's excrement. Is it firmer after the transitional period, or does your dog have the runs or even diarrhoea? Is your dog dropping excrement more frequently than they used to do, or are they letting off strong-smelling wind? How does the fur look after a longer period on canned food? If you have the impression that the dog's overall constitution is deteriorating on canned food diet, you may need to switch to home-cooked food or raw food if they are able to eat only soft food now.

Raw food

Feeding dogs with fresh meat is a continual point of debate, and there are a number of prejudices. Meanwhile, though, many dog-owners have switched to raw food and are seeing the benefits. With older dogs, one needs to bear in mind that they need more highly digestible proteins than younger dogs do. Because proteins are contained primarily in meat, this must be fed in a balanced proportion with vegetables. If your senior dog has problems maintaining their weight, it is important for the meat and fish to be easily digestible. Poultry is particularly suitable in this case. As the feeding of bones is also part of a raw food diet, a substitute needs to be found if the dog is no longer able to gnaw them. For this purpose, eggshells can be ground in a mortar and mixed with the food.

Less is more

Canine seniors who take less exercise also need less food. However, this food should contain everything the dog needs in terms of nutrients. For this reason, not the quantity but the quality of the food should be the focus. Therefore, feed your older dog at least twice a day, if possible, with a high-quality food that satisfies their appetite: if your dog is hungry – perhaps because you are be trying to make them diet – excessive production of gastric acid

can become extremely unpleasant for the dog and even lead to digestive system problems.

Balanced food for older dogs is designed so that the dog is satisfied by the ration that's intended for them, without putting on weight. Divide the indicated quantity for the daily ration into two and feed in two equally sized portions. If your dog isn't up to eating all their food, reduce the ration accordingly and offer them a little more at the next meal if need be. Elderly dogs, in particular, react in very different ways in this regard. Some prefer to be offered several smaller divided portions during the course of the day, while others eat an appropriate amount once a day and are happy with that.

If you feed dry food and have no other dogs, you can leave your senior dog's bowl where it is. There are dogs that don't like to gorge themselves all at once but divide up the food for themselves in the course of the day. The method of feeding that visibly does your senior good (condition of the fur, gleaming eyes, appropriate weight, satisfaction) is the right one!

Wow, that's a really fat dog!

No matter how good your intentions, you're not doing your older dog any favours if you trundle them through the autumn of their life as round as a ball. On the contrary: you're doing them damage! This is not only due to the burden on the bones and joints, which have to carry the excess weight, but also because of potential damage to the major organs, the heart, liver and kidneys, which can be fatal to your old dog. Additionally, the dog's

This old dog is unfortunately far too fat. (Photo: Tierfotoagentur/Schwerdtfeger)

movement and mobility will be even more restricted than it is already as a result of old age. So, do your dog a favour and do not over-feed them. Ensure that you provide an appropriate amount of a balanced diet and take action if the dog should happen to have become too fat as a result of illness or injury.

Diet schedule for canine seniors

If your older dog really does need to slim down, this must never be done suddenly. Excessive dieting increases the production of gastric acid, is a burden on heart, liver and kidneys, and may reduce your dog's performance even further for the period of the diet. If a dog is too fat, a physical examination and advice from a vet is essential. The vet will not only be able to recommend the right diet food, but will also check the dog's health on a regular basis during the slimming programme.

Do not under any circumstances schedule an excessive programme of exercise to be implemented overnight, either. Broaden the range of games and exercise gradually, and keep a close eye on what your dog can still do, or may be able to do again, and what may be too much of a burden for them. It does pay, though, to muster the patience and consistency to implement a diet programme for your senior. Many an older dog that was pre-sumed to be no longer able to run and jump has returned to being almost as happy and lively as they were in their younger years, by being taken through a well thought-out weight reduction programme.

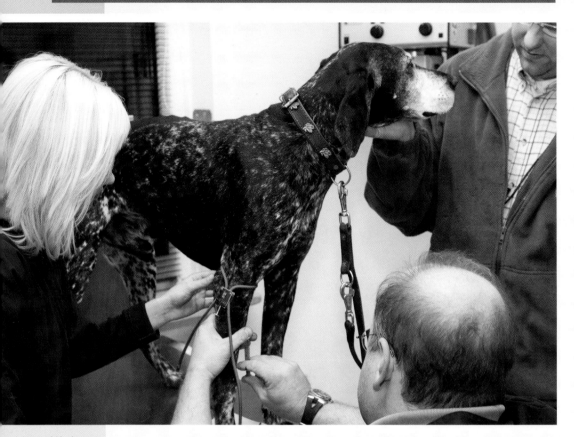

An annual blood test is to be recommended as part of the routine check at the vet's.

(Photo: JBTierfoto)

Living with the illnesses of canine old age

Getting old doesn't necessarily have to mean getting sick. For example, some old dogs stay healthy and lively to the end and then die in their sleep. Unfortunately, though, experience shows that these are the rare ones. This is why it is advisable to get used to the idea that an elderly dog may become ill. To make sure that you do the right thing at the right time, a regular health check on your canine senior by a trusted vet is no superfluous luxury. The earlier a geriatric disorder is detected and treated, the higher the chance that the dog's quality of life can be maintained and the disorder treated with success.

In many cases, the treatment of geriatric diseases can be integrated with everyday life. Regular dispensing of medication is sometimes necessary, but massages, canine physiotherapy exercises or the devising of a special diet can be included among the daily tasks that owners of elderly dogs will need to take on. Whether this becomes a burden, or adds a new dimension to the human-dog relationship, is up to you. Much joy can be had out of ensuring that your old dog is as well as they possibly can be.

For all who accept that the dog's old age is part of life together, it is a matter of course to take tender care of their companion even when, as a result of geriatric symptoms and disorders, times are not quite so easy. Unfortunately, it is often the case that dogs in their final phase of life are retired from service and written off, so to speak, because they no longer live up to their owners' notions. Fortunately, though, there are also people who are willing to adopt elderly dogs. In these homes, with the aid of loving care, old dogs often truly flourish and to a large extent recover from their illnesses. Thus, many a canine senior that wasn't expected to see another year has grown to be as old as the hills.

Preventive healthcare

It is wise to take an elderly dog to the vet twice a year and have them examined thor-oughly. The vet may be able to detect signs of illness early and will initiate the appropriate treatment. The necessary vaccination, professional teeth cleaning, nail clipping and a thorough check of the ears can also be performed during these appointments. You can take the worming and flea treatments for the next six months away with you as well. A routine blood test, which can shed light on symptoms of deficiency and changes in blood composition, is also to be recommended for older dogs. This may point to inflammatory or degenerative processes within the body that make swift intervention a necessity.

Vaccination

As with the young dog, the older animal receives protection against the prevailing infection pressure of traditional canine epidemic diseases by means of vaccination. In the ageing dog, particularly, the immune system is less resilient than it is in a young animal that's in rude health. This being the case, every senior dog should – after consultation with the vet – be vaccinated routinely. Both old and young dogs should be vaccinated against these diseases on a regular basis:

✓ Distemper
✓ Hepatitis
✓ Leptospirosis
✓ Parvovirus
✓ Parainfluenza virus

Worming

Worming treatments are just as important for old dogs as they are for young animals. The dog does possess a certain degree of natural defence against endoparasites, but this stands in direct correlation with the animal's overall immune efficiency, which may, in the older dog, be impaired. This is why worming treatments should be given on a regular basis to the old dog too. If the dog's excrement contains worms that can be seen with the naked eye, the assumption has to be that the dog is massively infested. Don't let it get to that stage!

Typical geriatric complaints

Signs of old age can turn into problems, complaints and, ultimately, illnesses. Sometimes old dogs can show signs of problems that began when they seemed healthy and lively. Untreated ear problems, for example, can lead to damage to the ear that may not become noticeable to its full extent until the dog reaches old age. If the ears are not cleaned regularly, this can lead to blockages and sticky ear wax; this results not only in a pronounced reduction in hearing, but the dog's sense of balance is also impaired. Many a case of unsteady walking or even swaying in dogs can be attributed to ear problems. A foul-smelling ear with discharge is always an alarm signal and requires a visit to the vet. There may be an infection present that requires treatment with antibiotics.

With the eyes, sometimes not only does the vision decline, but other eye complaints that never bothered the younger dog also arise. Some elderly dogs get so-called 'dry eyes': the resulting bacterial infection (kerato-conjunctivitis) is favoured by the fact that older dogs produce less tear fluid, or the composition of the tear film has altered to such an extent that it no longer provides sufficient protection to the eye. This infection is treated by the vet using an eye ointment.

In addition to ear and eye complaints, restricted mobility frequently causes old dogs a lot of discomfort. As with humans, bone condition deteriorates and tissue elasticity declines in dogs with age. We can take preventive measures against the complaints of old age by means of targeted feed-ing, but we cannot avoid them altogether. Although the supply of nutrients, such as calcium, strengthens the bones, it cannot halt symptoms of wear. For example, the cartilage lining of the joints wears down, potentially leading to arthrosis or arthritis. An accompanying breakdown of the musculature can lead to geriatric complaints that strongly restrict the dog's mobility. This is no reason, nevertheless, to let nature take its course. If you adapt your dog's surroundings to their altered living requirements and provide them with the appropriate treatment, they will be able to live a wonderful life even with geriatric complaints and continue to bring you a lot of pleasure.

Incontinence

Was your dog previously house-trained, and are you now suddenly finding a puddle or

Even if the dog's mobility is restricted as a result of geriatric complaints, with the right treatment they will still be able to live a happy and fulfilling life.

(Photo: Pinnekamp)

even a pile in the house now and again? Please do not get cross, because this is a sure sign of incipient incontinence. It is relatively rare for a dog to experience a change in behaviour that makes them start piddling in the house as a form of protest. In most cases physical causes stop the dog from doing their business where they've done it before, namely outside. For various reasons, it may no longer be possible for your dog to control their bladder and bowels sufficiently. Therefore, please never punish an old dog that has had an accident indoors. You can assume that it wasn't done deliberately.

There are various causes of incontinence. In bitches, the production of oestrogen declines in old age, and this potentially leads to incontinence. In this instance, treatment with medication is successful in many cases. In addition to urinary tract infections, which are treated with antibiotics, kidney disorders may be a cause of incontinence. If your dog is drinking an unusually large amount and needs to urinate frequently, this may be an indication of diabetes, which can occur in dogs as well as in humans.

What can you do? At all events, have your vet clarify and treat the cause of your dog's incontinence where possible. Take your dog out of doors regularly (possibly much more often than before), especially when they make it clear to you that they want to go out. Ensure that they are able to do their business as soon as they need to. If they are still able to hold on at all, it may be for much less time than when they were younger. Therefore, set up a spot where the dog can relieve themselves close to the house.

This could be a sandpit that you clean out regularly or, for smaller dogs, even a cat litter tray indoors that doesn't call for long distances to be covered in emergencies. In the event that none of the treatments is successful (which fortunately isn't the case too often), there is the option of putting a nappy on your dog indoors if they are leaving urine trails everywhere. Specialist stores carry nappies for dogs that are adapted to their size and make life together so much easier when treatment for incontinence is impossible, or is possible but not sufficient to solve the problem.

Bad breath and poor teeth

Bad breath in dogs can be associated with their food, but in most cases the cause is to be looked for directly in the mouth, on and around the teeth. A regular check-up and cleaning of the dental arch during a routine examination at the vet's should be a matter of course.

Some dogs allow their teeth to be cleaned without any problems, while some require sedation or anaesthesia in order to relax and submit to this necessary procedure. If you get your dog accustomed to regular dental care by rewarding them afterwards at an early stage, they will probably allow this to happen, trustingly, in old age.

If tooth damage has arisen, though, it is essential to have this treated by a vet who possesses thorough knowledge of the dental treatment of dogs. Comprehensive training courses are now available for these specialists, who are even able to adapt orthodontic instruments for dogs.

But have no fear – you will not have to have expensive gold inlays or ceramic bridges worth a month's salary produced for your dog – beauty is not the concern (in the case of show dogs, though, dental treatments are sometimes performed that even we humans would have second thoughts about); the primary concern with your old dog is that they don't have to suffer from painful teeth. Again and again, vets see dogs with infections in the mouth that must have put them through unbearable pain. Don't under any circumstances let things get that far; examine your dog's teeth and gums on a regular basis.

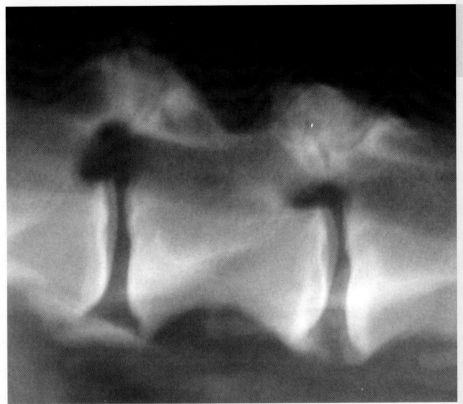

*This is what spondylosis
looks like on an X-ray.*

(Photo: JBTierfoto)

Disorders
of the locomotor system

In addition to age-related symptoms of
wear in the locomotor system, there are
disorders that may impair the dog's mobility even in their younger years. Essentially,
bigger breeds and those with inbred
anatomical abnormalities (for example, the
extremely long back of dachshunds or the
sloping hindquarters of German shepherds) tend to be more often affected than
smaller dogs and those with a more
favourable conformation.

Various forms of arthrosis and arthritis
can be observed in older dogs. Arthrosis
involves an alteration of the joints which,
combined with the reduction in cartilage
mass and an increase in bone mass, can
lead to immense problems with mobility.
Inflammation (arthritis) may arise, and
will likewise lead to pain and, subse-
quently, reluctance to move. Arthrosis of
the small joints in the spine is known as
spondylosis.

One of the widest known and most frequent manifestations of arthrosis is hip
dysplasia, where a genetically transmitted
malformation of the hip joint is present.
This can cause major pain even in young
dogs; in older dogs the sequences of movement of the hip joint are restricted more
and more severely by wear on the hips.
Affected dogs sit or lie down more often,
have great difficulty walking, or hobble

The state of health should be examined regularly in both large and small dogs. Big dogs such as mastiffs, unfortunately, tend to suffer from geriatric complaints more often and earlier in life than smaller breeds do.

(Photo: Tierfotoagentur/ Starick)

visibly. Dogs with this disorder should preferably not perform canine sports, and should avoid stairs and excessive strain. In addition to medication, which is used primarily to control pain, hip dysplasia can also be treated surgically. Physiotherapy for dogs supports muscle formation in the pelvic area and upper thighs, which provides support for the hip joint. This form of therapy has proven its worth in other disorders of the locomotor system, both following operations and in general sup-

port of mobility. Acupuncture, cartilage-strengthening food supplements, such as green-lipped mussel extracts, and, if required, the dispensing of anti-inflammatory medications can help dogs affected with arthrosis and arthritis to lead a pain-free and happy life.

In addition to diseases of the bones and joints, disorders of muscle can lead to impairments in mobility, which are primarily manifested as weakness in the hindquarters. Myopathy (degenerative muscle disease) occurs frequently in certain breeds (including German shepherds, boxers, Irish setters, huskies, Rhodesian ridgebacks and collies).

Many cases result from an auto-immune disorder which, in the worst cases, can lead to paralysis and death. Treatment methods that involve exercise (hydrotherapy), along with a special diet developed by an American vet, can, however, halt the progress of the disease in some cases.

Disorders of the major organs

The heart, liver and kidneys are the organs that are, unfortunately, frequently affected by disease in older dogs. Comprehensive diagnosis and treatment must always be performed by a vet; therefore I will restrict myself to the potential symptoms of organ diseases here.

A regular blood test will help to keep an eye on the dog's health, and in most cases will enable action to be taken in good time. Indications of internal disorders in the dog may be excessive drinking, refusal of food, weariness, frequent urination, a bloated belly, pronounced hair loss, and skin alterations. If your dog's behaviour has altered, for example they have become extremely agitated or conspicuously calm, you should take this as an indication for a thorough examination by the vet. Don't leave it too long, because disorders such as Cush-ing's syndrome (a disorder of the adrenal glands) or diabetes require immediate and targeted treatment by a vet.

Elderly dogs who become tired quickly, are coughing, and are perhaps even gasping for breath, may be suffering from a heart or lung disorder. Even though, in most cases, these disorders are, the dog's condition can be maintained in such a manner that the senior is able to live comfortably with the disease.

If a dog suffers from fluid retention as a result of a heart disorder, this likewise needs to be treated with medication. In most cases, the dog will receive diuretic medication in parallel with products that strengthen the heart and dilate the blood vessels.

Blood tests

Organ diseases such as inflammation of the kidneys or liver occur particularly in ageing dogs; therefore it should – as is the case in human medicine – be a matter of course to have a blood test performed on an elderly dog on an annual basis. This is not only because changes in the blood cells themselves (red and white blood counts) are immediately visible in the process, but you will also receive an immediate indication of the functions of the liver and kidneys. In most cases, early veterinary intervention in the incipient stages of restricted organ function enables the organ in question to be maintained for a considerable time. If you wait until clinically apparent symptoms appear before going to the vet and having a blood test performed, it may already be too late.

Becoming tired quickly and weariness can be signs of an internal disorder.

(Photo: Tierfotoagentur/ Schwerdtfeger)

Unfortunately, disorders of the reproductive organs are a frequent occurrence in older dogs. The commonest disorder in bitches is inflammation of the uterus (womb), the symptoms of which are vaginal discharge, frequent urination and increased temperature. If this disorder is detected soon enough and the uterus removed surgically, the prospects for recovery are good. Uncastrated male dogs often have problems with the prostate in old age. They eat poorly, move stiffly and find urination painful. Treatment with antibiotics can help, but in most cases castration is required.

Benign tumours

Many a dog-owner, when stroking their dog, has come to a horrified halt on discovering skin alterations, or small or large nodules, under the dog's fur. This isn't necessarily a tumour; a blocked sebaceous gland can also cause an easily palpable skin nodule which, after a while, will dry up and disappear exactly the way it came. Tumours are new formations of tissue that manifest themselves as lumps of various sizes. Benign tumours usually grow slowly, so particular caution is advised with rapidly growing lumps. Even benign tumours can degenerate during the course of their growth, and therefore become malignant. This is why it is important, in addition to arrang-ing an examination by your vet, to watch the lump closely, measure its growth if possible and intervene as soon as required. The vet should decide whether a benign tumour needs to be removed surgically. They will also want to observe the lump on a regular basis and check it for various symptoms. If the lump can be moved about freely and is lying directly in or under the skin, this is commonly a relatively good sign as it can be assumed that the lump is not infiltrative, i.e. it is not growing into the surrounding tissue.

Malignant tumours: cancer

If a tissue growth begins to take up more space and if growth into the surrounding tissue can be observed, a malignant tumour is commonly implicated. This disease is generally described as cancer. However, a malignant tumour need not be a death sentence for a dog. With early detection and specific treatment, even dogs with cancer are often able to be discharged with a clean bill of health. If possible, malignant tumours should be removed surgically at an early stage. However, the feasibility and success of the operation depends on the location of the tumour. A tumour that one of my whippets had on

How to administer medication

Most medications in powder or tablet form can be given to the dog as follows: grind the tablets in a mortar and mix the resulting powder with a little butter. Place this little ball on the back part of the tongue and then hold the dog's mouth closed (without trapping their cheeks!).

The butter will melt on the tongue straight away and the dog will swallow automatically. You can also 'pack' capsules this way, using a little more butter. With some dogs this technique also works using liver pâté, but this has the disadvantage that it doesn't melt on the tongue.

Common benign tumours are wart-like skin tumours or benign melanomas, which may manifest on the skin as little black nodules. Benign growths can also occur in the dog's mouth. Gum tumours, which are commonly benign, should be surgically removed by the vet and sent to a laboratory for histological examination (tissue examination under the microscope) to be on the safe side.

his back had degenerated, and it suddenly grew to the size of a plum within days. As at least one centimetre of healthy tissue needs to be removed around the tumour, a lot of skin was removed from the whippet's back during the operation. His 'jacket' became tighter and tighter, and the scar was under severe strain. This tumour returned twice more after the first operation and was removed successfully during the third operation. Everything healed well, and the dog lived to the age

Long-haired breeds need
to be checked particularly
carefully for potential
tissue growths.

(Photo: Tierfotoagentur/
Richter)

of fourteen. Common types of cancer seen in older dogs are tumours on the mammary glands in bitches, and tumours in the dog's mouth and throat, but also liver carcinoma and tumours of the spleen.

There are now various forms of treatment for cancer in dogs that are similar to those used in humans. In addition to complex operations, chemotherapy or radiotherapy may be an option, and may prolong the dog's life. Please always weigh up the pros and cons of such intensive treatment methods and consider whether an appropriate quality of life is assured for your companion both during and after the treatment.

The visually impaired or blind dog

A clouding of the lens can be observed in many old dogs. In most cases, this can be attributed to cataracts, which can greatly restrict the dog's vision as time passes. An operation is possible, but is not appropriate in all cases. A rarer occurrence is glaucoma, which is painful for dogs, as for humans; medication is essential for this illness. In both cases, you should discuss the correct course of treatment with your vet.

If old dogs have poor vision or can no longer see at all, there are many ways to help them. We can arrange the dog's living environment in such a manner that they can cope, despite their disability. Even a 'guide dog for the blind dog' can be a source of support: training can usually be dispensed with, because, when several dogs are kept together, it's often entirely a matter of course that a blind dog will orientate towards its seeing

canine pals. When it's necessary to leave known territory, the dog will need their human to guide them safely through the world.

For this it is essential for human and dog to have a good relationship and for the dog to be able to build up sufficient trust to follow their human. Imagine the world as your visually impaired or blind dog will encounter it, and never under any circumstances expose them to situations that they are unable to cope with owing to their disability. This includes, for example, confrontation with other dogs, but also with strange people and potentially boisterous children.

Given that the dog cannot see what is happening, they may feel threatened, hass-led or confused. Who would blame them if they growled or snapped in such circumstances?

Adapting the surroundings

If your dog gradually went blind in their habitual surroundings, they probably won't have too many difficulties. They will take their usual routes inside the house and orientate themselves to familiar smells, distances and noises. On the other hand, a house move with a visually impaired or blind dog is somewhat more problematic and will require a lot of empathy from the dog's owner. As far as possible, make sure that there is nothing in the way of your old dog on the paths that they are going to take routinely in the (new) house.

Place the food and water bowl somewhere that's easily accessible, and remind your dog of this place until they are able to find the way there on their own. Keep the feeding and watering place exactly where it is, just like your dog's long-estab-

This little dog needed to have an eye removed because of an illness. However, she can still see well enough with the other eye and copes astonishingly well.

(Photo: JBTierfoto)

lished spots for resting in, so that they can rely on finding everything in the same place again and again.

Communicating with the visually impaired or blind dog

The most important prerequisite for effective communication with visually impaired dogs is a good relationship between human and dog. The dog must be able to muster sufficient trust to follow you, and have the feeling of being in good hands with you.

You need to work with audible signals or tactile information (touching the dog) when communicating with a visually impaired or blind dog.

In this new situation, this is a learning process which requires one thing above all: patience! Do not become impatient if your dog doesn't understand you straight away. Maybe your signal was unclear or different from last time? Try to use the same signal consistently all the time, so that your dog can rely on it. If you have conditioned your dog to respond to a whistle, this is particularly helpful now, especially on walks. Whistle when the dog has moved too far away or is potentially running in the wrong direction. Then wait until they come to you and reward them. If you merely want to let the dog know where you are at the moment without requiring them to come to you, you can try hand-clapping. The dog will then be able to locate you more easily.

If your dog has always communicated with you via eye contact, they now need to learn to listen attentively. Talk to the dog quietly and affectionately and offer them clear and comprehensible commands that make sense in everyday life. Backing up the audible signal with a friendly touch will allow your dog to understand what you're expecting of them more effectively.

Keep your dog on the lead more often than before, letting them run free only when there is no imminent danger and the surroundings are familiar to them. Think from their side of things when something approaches you that the dog is unable to see (bicycles, cars), or when your dog runs up to something they haven't registered yet. Do not allow them to 'run into' risks or mistakes, but use a 'word of warning' ('Careful!' 'Look out!'), so that your dog knows when danger is imminent.

Point your dog in the direction of a place where they are able to run or play out of the reach of danger, and protect them from surprise encounters with other dogs, boisterous children and adults who may try to stroke the dog without warning. Always allow your dog to sniff the person first, and accept it if they turn away and refuse further contact. Position yourself protectively in front of your dog, and fend off attackers when it is necessary, but do not pick up the dog. Naturally, you should never put yourself at risk on behalf of your dog and pick a fight with other dogs. Try to take defensive action well in advance if a difficult situation looks likely to develop.

The hearing-impaired or deaf dog

Impaired hearing or deafness can arise as a result of ear disorders, but also as a normal symptom of old age. As a result of wear on the sensory cells (hair cells) inside the ear, hearing ability declines, potentially even leading to creeping deafness in very old dogs. You will notice it by the way your dog no longer reacts to you when they can't see you, or stops running up to you expectantly as soon as you clatter the food bowl. It goes without saying that existing disorders of the ear need to be treated. Deterioration of hearing ability can perhaps be halted by treatment, but not reversed. You therefore need to learn how to cope with it together.

Communicating with the hearing-impaired or deaf dog

On walks, but indoors as well, you will need to use manual signals in order to communicate with your dog. Fetch the dog when they are somewhere else in the house in the process of sleeping through dinner time. Touch them carefully and perform a hand movement which you can then use in the same way every time you want to let your dog know that you want them to follow you.

It makes sense to carry a clearly visible toy that you can use to encourage your dog to pay attention to you. You can then make the dog aware of you when you want

When the human has limitations too, trust and effective communication are particularly important to ensure that the walk together is a success.

(Photo: Tierfotoagentur/ Richter)

them to come to you. Reward them afterwards with a brief game with this toy, or with a treat.

Remember that you won't be able to call your dog when they run in the wrong direction, or when they are running up to other people who perhaps won't welcome the approach of a dog. You may therefore need to run along behind or wait until the dog comes back of their own volition. Depending on where you go for your walks, it may be best to allow the dog to walk on a flexi-lead. When choosing a place to let your dog run free, give preference to fenced land that provides a clear overview so that your companion can let off steam to their heart's content without risk.

Dementia in dogs

Dog Alzheimer's? Yes, there is such a thing. The symptoms of so-called cognitive disorders (CD) in dogs really are comparable with the striking features seen in humans, whose mental functions can deteriorate rapidly within a very short space of time.

Dogs with such disorders sometimes show very altered behaviours, but the cause of such behaviours may lie in another disorder. This is why it is very important to have the vet exclude other physical disorders before making a diagnosis of dementia. In many cases, it is not easy to discover the reasons behind a dog's altered behaviour. If the dog is uneasy, restless or easily provoked, this can be an indication of a degenerative process in the brain – but it doesn't have to be. If your dog starts whining in var-

ious situations, it needs to be confirmed that they are not in any pain that requires treatment. The reason behind barking for no apparent reason should also be investigated. Blind or deaf dogs sometimes bark in situations of which they are uncertain, even if they never did it before. Sudden incontinence can have other causes, too, as can unusually aggressive behaviour or difficulties with climbing stairs.

However, if the dog suddenly stops, disorientated, in the hallway and stands there facing the wall until rescued, this may indeed be a sign of a dementia-related disorder. Other signs of confusion require a more detailed investigation: some dogs who used to love going on car journeys suddenly exhibit previously unknown fears – they tremble, bark and possibly urinate; others seem disorientated, fearful or apathetic in places they've often visited before. There are also dogs who no longer recognise their human, or stop reacting to commands that they've responded to for their entire lifetime.

If, after comprehensive neurological investigation, the vet has made a diagnosis of dementia, all is not lost. It is possible to slow the degenerative process with the aid of prescription medication that may also reduce the symptoms of the disorder. Use of sedatives in low doses can also help the dog to emerge from fearful states and live a relatively normal life for quite a while. In this case, health check-ups by the vet at regular intervals are essential in order to observe the effect of the medication, and to be able to intervene if the dog's condition deteriorates rapidly.

There is now a type of dry food available that has been specifically developed for dogs with symptoms of dementia. It

Some dogs with dementia will look at their human, but fail to recognise them. This is precisely the time when they need our help the most.

(Photo:Tierfotoagentur/ Schwerdtfeger)

is supposed to counter the degenerative processes in the brain and can be fed even when the disorder is advanced.

With this disorder it is necessary to focus strongly on the dog's needs. It may be that your dog can no longer be left alone, even in their familiar environment. Sometimes it helps to keep the dog in one specific room only, preferably one where they have always felt at ease. Ensure that the temperature is pleasant there, that a cosy basket, water and food

are available, and that the valuable Persian rug won't have to go straight to the tip because the dog could no longer control their bladder or bowels. Sometimes it helps to switch on the radio or let another calm dog into the room with the old dog. The time may come, though, when your dog requires nursing and round-the-clock care. If they do, it is now time to consider whether the dog is still enjoying an adequate quality of life.

Our old whippet who suffered from cognitive disorder still had a great time in the house and garden during the day, together with our other dogs. However, the situation changed as soon as the sun went down: totally disorientated, he would then spend hours howling away and it was impossible to calm him down. This is a phenomenon that is also seen in human patients. Daylight has a clear influence on the patient's state of health and orientation status. When our dog's disorientated phases started extending into the daytime and there were only tiny time-frames when he was still looking happy, we had to make a decision that is difficult for everyone in such a situation: we had to have him put to sleep.

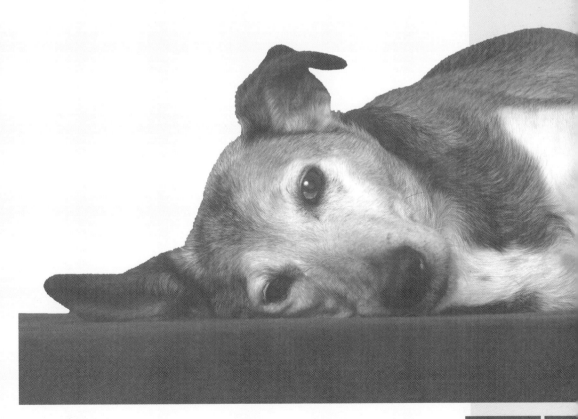

It's a good thing that you usually can't tell exactly when the time will come to say goodbye.

(Photo: Tierfotoagentur/ Schubbel)

Room in your heart for ever:
Saying goodbye

There are people who won't get a dog in the first place because they know that they'll have to say goodbye to them one day. Unfortunately, there are also people who give away their old dog as soon as they have problems so that they can replace them with a young one straight away. But, happily, there are many people for whom the death of a beloved pet is just as much a part of life as puppyhood is. If we have led a wonderful and fulfilled life together, this may not make the goodbye any easier but it will give us many precious memories. Every dog is different, and some of them cause a lot of tears to flow because the gap that they leave behind is so large.

It has been my experience that it's easier to keep plenty of room in your heart for your dog if you live through the moment of farewell consciously and fill it with dignity.

When the dog dies suddenly

The unexpected death of a dog is certainly difficult to cope with, especially if your friend was not yet old and you were totally unprepared. An accident, a fatal disease or even death on the operating table can be the cause of a dog's unpredicted death. Even if you were unable to be there when it happened, it will perhaps do you good if you take the time to say goodbye.

If your dog is at home, you can lay them in their basket, cover them up and let your tears flow freely. If they have passed away somewhere else, you may have the opportunity to take them home with you. If you don't wish to do this, perhaps a photo from better times and lighting a candle will help you to calm down and reflect on what has happened.

Do not force yourself straight back into your everyday routine – a dog is a family member, and it is justifiable to feel extremely sad about the death. Children find little rituals particularly helpful when trying to cope with this situation. They are often much more open to them than adults are. Don't be afraid, even as an adult, to follow a little ritual after the death of your canine friend.

When treatment can no longer help

There will be time for a dignified farewell when your dog is so ill that, though treatment may be able to ensure that they are not in pain, improvement is no longer possible. If the vet has to tell you this, it usually takes a while to sink in: your beloved companion is going to die in the not-too-distant future. Your vet will be able to estimate how your dog is doing, and will know what options you have in order to make their final days pleasant.

Perhaps they need a particularly high degree of warmth, certain medications, or several small meals a day. Even though, just by looking at your dog, you're bound to be continually reminded that soon they'll no longer be with you, enjoy this time. Go with them (if they are still able) to places where they always enjoyed being, spend a lot of time with them and lavish attention upon them. Why shouldn't they lie alongside you on the sofa, even if perhaps they weren't allowed to do so before? Why shouldn't you slip your old dog tit-bits now and again?

Give your dog particularly tender loving care: brush them daily – if they like it – bring them back an especially nice piece of meat from the butcher's if they no longer really enjoy eating, and make them the centre of your (family) life.

When there are other animals in the household who are very fond of their doggy pal, you should be aware that they will probably mourn too when the dog is no longer there.

(Photo: Tierfotoagentur/ Schwerdtfeger)

Many dogs really perk up again at times like these. Suddenly, for a few days or weeks perhaps, they'll have unheard of energy again, bark at the postman the way it should be done, chase the neighbour's cat up the tree, and pinch that cake off the table.

If you notice as time goes by that these energies are declining, then try to be honest with yourself: is your dog's life still dignified and happy, or are they possibly suffering, in pain, and unable to walk any more? Talk to your vet so that they can appraise your dog's condition objectively.

A difficult decision: having your dog put to sleep

Few dogs die a natural death. Though we have intensive medicine for dogs as well, which can prolong their lives, care for 'bedridden' dogs has its limits. If a dog is no longer able to stand up, control their bladder and bowels, and otherwise do what is typical for dogs, it is time to consider whether you should have them put to sleep. However, try to avoid dragging your domestic companion to the vet in this state. The strain of the journey, the natural apprehension at the clinic, and your agitation as well, will unsettle your dog in this situation and may turn their final journey into a hectic muddle. Even though it's bound to cost more, ask your vet to come to your home in order to put the dog to sleep in their familiar surroundings. If a trip to the clinic can't be avoided, always make an appointment with your vet outside of clinic hours so that you and your dog are not exposed to the general bustle and the well-intended comments from other pet owners.

Being there for your friend

Do not leave the canine friend who has been with you for many years all alone in their final hour. In most cases, putting a dog to sleep is a serene and almost peaceful procedure, during which your dog should sense your closeness. Feel free to hold their paw, and don't be ashamed of your tears in front of the vet – these will only show how much you love your dog.

When?

The vet will suggest a time to you when they are able to visit. Choose the moment so that the whole family can take plenty of time to say goodbye to the dog – also so that nobody has an appointment, football training or dinner with friends straight afterwards. If you can manage it, take time off work. It will be a difficult day, but also a day for coming closer together in your grief over the death of your dog. If the vet is able to come in the late morning (maybe after clinic hours), you won't have to wait all day, but you will still have a few last hours to spend with your dog. There will still be time in the afternoon to keep the dog with you for

a little while longer, pick a lovely bouquet of flowers and bury your dog, if that is what you have chosen.

Where?

Preferably where your dog always enjoyed lying. There is no reason to banish the dying senior to the cellar all of a sudden, and the procedure of putting a dog to sleep doesn't require a tiled bathroom either. The dog can simply remain lying in their familiar basket, covered with their favourite blanket and surrounded by all those who wouldn't want to leave their good friend alone at such a moment. During the procedure of putting your dog to sleep, at some point they will produce urine and excrement. Therefore, expect to have to throw away the blanket your dog was lying on afterwards, or put it in an extremely hot wash. Personally, I think it's important to let the dog lie on their usual

blanket, and would even sacrifice a particularly luxurious dog blanket with all my love at a moment like this.

How?

Whether it takes place at the clinic or at home, the putting to sleep procedure is always similar and, performed by a caring vet, is no terrible event. The dog may have an indwelling cannula inserted into the vein. An injection into the muscles of the hindquarters is a possible alternative. Via the cannula, or intramuscularly, the dog may receive a narcotic which, as before an operation, will induce a safe deep anaesthesia. This ensures that they won't notice anything of the final putting to sleep procedure. An overdose of a

narcotic (barbiturate) is now given into the vein. This will lead to swift heart and respiratory failure, from which the dog will die immediately.

If the dog is very old and has poor circulation and if the vein is no longer accessible, an intracardiac injection (into the heart) or intrapulmonary injection (into the lungs) may be necessary. Given that the dog is under full anaesthesia, they won't notice anything at this time.

Dogs frequently open their mouths once more and breathe audibly for the last time before finally passing into the next world. If a narcotic is used, you need not fear that the dog will twitch or convulse. Your dog will lie in their basket totally relaxed and look as though they are sleeping.

It really does look as though he's only sleeping. Tender rituals such as a fresh bouquet of flowers and a warm blanket will turn the sad occasion into a dignified farewell.

(Photo: Fritschy)

Mikey in the gardens of remembrance at Dignity Pet Crematorium in Hampshire.

(Photo reproduced with kind permission by Dignity Pet Crematorium, a member of the APPCC.)

Pet burial and pet cemeteries

Your vet will probably offer to take a dog that they have just put to sleep away with them for cremation at a pet crematorium for an additional fee. There is a great deal of confusion over this service due to the legal requirement for animals to be handled under the waste regulations and the expectations you may have for your pet's cremation. Most vets do not understand this and it is best to ask for written con-

firmation of the procedures involved. The Association of Private Pet Cemeteries & Crematoria publish a trading standard by which you may compare different services. It is often best to deal directly with the crematorium but always ensure you are getting the service you want and do not be misled by appearances. Your pet bereavement facility will be able to make arrangements for collection if you are not able to take your dog or there are some pet undertaker services that will arrange all the details. If you have an individual crema-

No two dogs are alike. It is always unfair to make comparisons.

(Photo: Tierfotoagentur/ Fischer)

tion and the ashes returned you may wish to keep them or scatter at your chosen location. They may also be strewn or buried at a memorial garden at a pet cemetery or crematorium.If you do not like the idea of cremation then there are various options for burying you dog with dignity. Burial is allowed on your own land where your dog lived as long as it is not prevented by local by laws. Pet cemeteries exist all over the country and range from formally laid out plots to woodland burials where trees may be planted in remembrance. Pet cemeteries vary in appearance so always try to see it first before you decide to have your dog buried there. You want to ensure you have a final resting place that you are happy with and that you may visit and enjoy the memories of your beloved pet in peace.

A new dog?

A deserted basket, the unused lead in the hall, and no boisterous canine welcome when you arrive home make the initial period without your dog a difficult time. If you have several dogs, there are always the others to be looked after; if you had only one dog, the absence will be even more striking. Only you can decide whether to take on a new dog straight away or wait a while. There's no right or wrong here, just your feelings, pure and simple. And if you want a new dog, they are bound to enter your life at just the right time. You will definitely not forget their predecessor because of this. A new dog will never replace the old one, they will merely be their successor and will win a place in your heart that's entirely their own.

(Photo: Pinnekamp)

Thank You

My thanks go to Dr Jochen Becker for his veterinary advice concerning this book. I also thank the old dogs who have been part of my life so far, for our wonderful time together.

Addresses

Veterinary dentists:
Addresses of vets with an additional qualification in animal dental care can be requested via the British Veterinary Dental Association: www.bvda.co.uk

Scented tubes for scenting games and other interactive toys:
www.companyofanimals.co.uk
www.traininglines.co.uk

Plaque Off®:
Available from numerous online suppliers of veterinary pharmaceuticals.
www.vetuk.co.uk
www.medicanimal.com

Nappies for dogs:
www.dog-nappy.co.uk

Soft blankets and beds for dogs with arthritis:
www.catsandcanines.co.uk

Pet burial and cremation:
www.appcc.org.uk

Pet bereavement support service:
www.scas.org.uk/Petlossandbereavement
Phone 0800 0966606

Support for people who are ill and their pets:
www.cinnamon.org.uk
Phone 01736 757900

Further reading

Bessant, Claire, Neville, Peter, Viner,
Bradley and Duin, Nancy
How to Give your
Dog a Longer and Healthier Life
Smith Gryphon

Bleby, John and Bishop, Gerald
The Dog's Health from A to Z
David and Charles

Bowers, John and Youngs, David
The Dog Owner's
Veterinary Handbook
Crowood Press

Hallgren, Anders:
Mental Activation
Cadmos Books

Matthews, Jane:
Losing a Pet
Smallbooks

Röder, Nicole:
Whose Sofa is it anyway?
Cadmos Books

Sondermann, Christina:
Playtime for your Dog
Cadmos Books

Tellington-Jones, Linda
Getting in Touch with your Dog
(TTouch), Kenilworth Press

Zaitz, Manuela:
Trick School for Dogs
Cadmos Books

Index

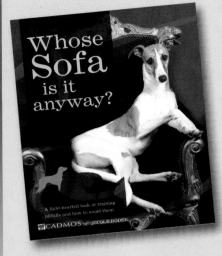

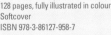